Testimor

"...a very easy to read book with some top tips..."

"...Jonny links his own experience with an openness and honesty that gives his ideas an authenticity that resonates strongly and leaves you reflecting on your own experience."

"A top read from a top practitioner."

Keith Towler - former Children's Commissioner

"…Interesting, informative and enlightening read."

"Strength comes from facing ones own weaknesses…Jonny has learnt this the hard way and has had the courage to record his findings."

"A MUST read for all those working in the caring industry…"

Foster carer and former magistrate

—

"Detailed self-help guides and manuals work for some, but what we often lack is something straightforward that sets it out simply, tells it as it is and from the voice of experience. Jonny's book does that."

Policy adviser and youth justice researcher

"...This book immediately struck a chord on several levels."

"I think this book will be a great read for practitioners across the spectrum - from newly qualified to those who need to remind themselves how important it is not to lose sight of how important self-care is."

"Great stuff Jonny!"

Social worker and children's services training officer

Contents...

Here's what's coming:

JonnyMatthew.com
Promoting recovery for troubled young people...

1. Intro

People who care for others tend to be neglectful of one thing

Themselves.

There's just something about the caring instinct that's anything but self-centred.

I learnt this to my cost a number of years ago when I pretty much burned out. I ended up having a few weeks off work and had to re-assess the impact of the job and how I was coping.

Or not coping, as it happened!

From that unfortunate episode I came away with some key lessons about the way our kind of work can affect us.

Among these were:

* Learning to recognise how we are feeling.

* Taking practical steps to stay well.

* Things agencies can do to support staff better.

Basically, this is a multi-pronged approach to help us work to our best and provide the optimum service to the kids we work with.

This little book is a composite of material I've written over the last couple of years on JonnyMatthew.com.

It draws on my experience of working with children and young people in social work, sexual abuse, youth justice and secure care.

I've also drawn on the wisdom and experience of others who've been kind enough to share their learning with me.

I hope you find it useful and gain some insights to help you work well and stay well!

Cheers,

Jonny

2. Looking After No.1

Facing the facts

I've recently had a couple of days off and I'm still tired.

Maybe it's the late nights or the chocolate-filled days. Or maybe it's just being 50 years old!

But perhaps some of it is due to the impact of working with troubled young people for 20-odd years – it can certainly take its toll.

Once again I'm looking in the mirror asking, "Do I look after myself enough?"

Do you?

Playing with fire

You know what they say? If you play with fire, sooner or later you're going to get burnt!

It's now very well established that working with other people's problems has an impact. Whilst there is joy and success in what we do, there can be negative stuff too.

Sometimes very negative.

Psychologists have various terms for it, including:

- Vicarious Traumatisation.

- Secondary Traumatic Stress.

- Compassion Fatigue Syndrome.

Whatever the label, the result is the same. The worker suffers difficulties through helping other people deal with theirs.

The first step to avoiding the negative impact of our work is to accept that it can happen. We can be affected, badly.

Before we can put the necessary things in place to protect and sustain ourselves, we must first accept that we have the potential to be impacted.

3. The bullet-proof worker

Is there such a thing?

When I first started to work with children with sexualised histories, I thought I could pretty much take anything that came my way.

I'd been around the block. I'd seen and heard some pretty heavy duty things over the years and never really been impacted that much by it all. Or so I thought.

This led, slowly, to an unrealistic sense of my own resilience. Basically, I thought I could handle whatever the work, the kids, their families or the agency could throw at me.

I was wrong.

This kind of attitude - spoken or unspoken - can be present on two different levels:

- The personal or individual level.

- The organisational or workplace level.

When we start to feel a little fragile we can put ourselves under pressure to keep going. We don't want to be seen to be flagging.

Or the place we work - the people, the culture, the boss - can leave us feeling we have to carry on regardless.

It can help to take a little time out to think through where the pressures are coming from.

ACTION POINT:

Ask yourself: who exactly is applying the pressure on   you to cope - to keep going even when you know things are getting hard?

Are you putting yourself under pressure?

Is your agency or workplace doing it?

4. Macho work culture

The need to resist!

We've established that working with troubled children and young people is real work. It's hard work. It takes its toll, if we're not very careful.

So we need our workplace to be supportive, not macho…

But some working cultures aren't healthy.

Before we know it we find ourselves under pressure. Under pressure to cope, to stick at it and not to make waves.

Nothing makes waves like being off sick though, right? So we keep going.

Even when we know we should stop and take stock.

Workplace pressures

It's not the office that applies these pressures, obviously. It's the other factors that are present in every workplace:

* Staff groups

11

- Working cultures

- Individual people or managers

Each of these in different ways can pressure us to appear capable, to cope alone and quietly. To keep our feelings to ourselves and just "get on with it."

Here's an example

I recall the episode very clearly:

We had just been involved in dealing with some very challenging and aggressive behaviour from a teenage boy.

During the incident a colleague of mine was assaulted – he was punched squarely in the face. Very hard.

I know it was hard because I heard it from 20 feet away when my back was turned. I also saw the welt above his eye afterwards.

I could see that my colleague was not only physically affected by the assault, he was also emotionally affected. He was shaking. He couldn't stand still. His voice was emotional.

All this is normal and to be expected.

What wasn't normal – or at least shouldn't be – was what happened next.

Cultural collateral damage

I suggested that he take some time out and have a coffee – at the very least. Or, if he needed to, that he should go home and rest. He was still shaking.

My plan - in my efforts to be a supportive manager - was to allow him time to wind down and return to calm again. We would then deal with the aftermath of the incident later.

Staff welfare comes first, right? Not here.

This is what he said:

> "I'm alright, it's nothing. I've had a lot worse than this in rugby training."

Oh dear!…

ACTION POINT:

Ask yourself: what excuses do I make - to myself or others - when I know things are starting to get tough?

Being honest with ourselves is the first step to changing habits that keep us caught in the macho culture.

5. Remembering the "why"

Staff and kids deserve better

Dealing with issues and decisions is easier when we keep our focus on why were are doing this work in the first place.

As the saying goes:

"If you've lost your way it's probably because you've forgotten your why."

The incident in this example took place in an environment where there was an unspoken pressure to cope.

The cultural pressure was so strong that it persuaded an intelligent, capable and mature adult to make a bad decision.

He made the decision because the culture told him that…

- To admit feeling shaken was to admit weakness.

- To go home following such an incident was tantamount to failure.

His injury, his heightened emotional state and his mental fragility at that moment meant he needed a break. At least!

But the cultural pressure in that workplace - and maybe his own internal pressure - pushed him to keep going. To put a brave face on it and crack on.

Why we must ditch the macho

Here are some of the reasons why we must challenge such workplace cultures:

> Setting a good example to children – If we are to really help troubled kids to recover, we should model normal responses.

This must include normal emotional responses. Not that we should bare our feelings in front of kids. But for them to know that this man – this strong, muscly, capable man – was upset and needed some time out – would have balanced the macho assumptions beautifully.

Instead it was hidden.

The kids in his care would have been party to a great example of good practice if he'd responded differently.

Like the rest of us, children more easily learn from what they experience than they do from what they're told.

Seeing someone get their priorities right in practice is worth ten thousand words of lecturing or written instruction.

It's the repetition of just these kinds of experiences that teaches children - eventually - to look after themselves.

> Good self-care – If we are ever properly to be sensitive to children, we also must be sensitive to our own needs.

Reflection is one of the greatest assets a practitioner with troubled children can have.

Knowing when you're affected is a safeguard for the children and for ourselves – it means we'll be more likely to stay the course and be healthy doing it.

Once again, the children we serve will learn valuable lessons when they observe us getting it right. After all, we want them to stay the course too. How better to aid this process than by showing them how to look after number 1?

The kids need us to be healthy – Looking after ourselves ensures we're rested, ready and available to respond to their needs.

Constant changes of worker, staff absences and other inconsistencies are made much worse when self-care is lacking.

The kids we deal with are particularly unsettled when things are unstable and inconsistent. Staff absence brings both.

With high need children, we all need to be on our mettle. All the time. That way the young people get the best possible service we can offer.

And that's what this is all about.

This is our "why."

ACTION POINT:

Ask yourself: am I working to my optimum potential at the moment?

If not, what's stopping me from being a good example by caring for myself first?

6. Strategic reasons to ditch the macho

The healthy workplace

As well as the obvious personal benefits, there are also some good strategic reasons to foster a caring culture at work:

- Duty of care – Agencies have a duty of care to all staff. Those with management responsibilities should bear this in mind when addressing their workplace culture.

- Sickness absence – Looking after staff and fostering an openness about worker stress will alleviate pressure and lead to healthier staff teams. This in turn will reduce sickness absence. Once again, young people benefit from the consistency this brings.

- Spreading the load – the best people to empathise with impact issues are our colleagues – they work in it too! But when people are off sick the burden falls on those left behind, increasing their load. This is how sickness cycles begin.

Absence begets more absence – wise management will avoid this by promoting a caring culture at work.

Focused workplace

So there are lots of reasons – personal and strategic – why macho work cultures should be resisted.

At the end of it all, though, agencies and workers exist to help the children and young people who come to our attention. That's our raison d'être.

With proper staff care and a working culture of open reflection the children and young people receive the best possible input we have to give. We are all free and able to focus on what matters.

ACTION POINT:

Ask yourself: what do I need to do differently in order to avoid being affected by a macho work culture?

7. Beating burnout

An object lesson

My wife and my friends will tell you the truth about me – "He's a bit ADHD," or, " He's very high energy."

Someone saying, "I don't know how you get it all done" isn't that unusual for me. It's who I am.

So when things went pear-shaped and I got sick and just stopped dead in my tracks, they were worried.

I was worried. This wasn't just highly unusual. The degree of exhaustion - mentally and physically - was quite frightening.

Here's why:

- I was exhausted but couldn't get to sleep.

- Wasn't eating properly (and I like my grub!).

- I stopped doing the things I love in my spare time.

- Felt weak and drained and had no energy.

- Headaches, irritability, lots of neck and shoulder pain.

- I couldn't face the thought of work, let alone actually doing it.

- Yet I found myself ruminating about kids, cases and decisions...

- My body ached, my mind was numb and I had no motivation or energy for anything.

Burnout.

Decisions, deadlines and dilemmas

Like most people, I was having the usual management supervision as part of my everyday working routine. It was regular, well organised and sensitive.

But when it comes to dealing with the stress of this kind of work, management supervision doesn't cut the mustard.

It's mainly about decisions, deadlines and dilemmas. All necessary, of course. But what we also need is help with the way the work affects us personally.

That's where clinical supervision really scores.
The focus is on how we and the work connect.
How we affect the work and how the work affects us.
It's a two-way street.

...and dosh

Now, you and I know that organisations don't easily part with their cash. Particularly in these days of austerity.

Later on we'll look a bit more closely at clinical supervision and the role it can play in staff welfare and beating burnout.

In the meantime, how can we get the support we need that goes over and above our normal supervision?

Here are a couple of things that might help (though won't solve it on their own!)...

- Set up a peer supervision session – say once a month? Do it at lunchtime if diaries don't allow a formal slot during work time.

- Work impact as a supervision agenda item – Ask your management supervisor to add to the agenda a discussion about the impact of the work. Then suggest it gets discussed each time you meet.

- **Set up a mastermind group** – A group of people with similar work interests – a kind of out-of-work-time peer support group.

None of these will replace proper clinical supervision.

But they can help by creating a forum to discuss the impact of the work. It can also help to hear about other people's efforts to cope. Foster carers are often good at this kind of informal peer support - the rest of us would do well to learn from them.

Maybe the greatest advantage of all is the potential for these kinds of peer-led forums to have a positive impact on staff culture.

ACTION POINT:

Ask yourself: what more could I do to support others at work in order to help everyone feel more supported?

What first step could I take to begin the process of doing this?

8. Practical hacks

Stuff we can all do to help ourselves

After my brush with burnout I got to thinking.

I really went back to the drawing board to see what changes I might need to make in order to avoid a repeat of the whole sorry episode.

It was both an enlightening and humbling experience.

Humbling because I realised how much I'd been affected. Enlightening because some of the steps I took were really very simple.

But their effects were profound. Here are some of the things I did to help myself:

> Spread my leave from work more evenly throughout the year – I was taking bigger blocks of leave in the summer and at Christmas, but the gaps in between were too long.

Planning time off more frequently, but for less time, made a positive difference. Physically I recovered more quickly. Psychologically, it was never too long before my next leave period.

For foster carers, for example, I recommend that you insist on regular, predictable respite periods. Try it, you might be surprised…

> **Plan in some down-time during the week and stick to it** – I decided that on Wednesday of each week, I wouldn't see any children.

I would use that day to complete referrals, catch up on recording, plan the next phase of work, attend meetings, conduct supervision with colleagues, etc.

It was busy. Very busy. But not with dealing in the challenges of other people's trauma.

On the occasions when I was less disciplined, or I had to see someone on a Wednesday, I noticed the difference.

See how you can break up your work in a similar way.

> **Leave work at work** – I had got into some bad habits. For example, I was bringing work-related reading home almost every night – books, journals, research papers…

I love to read and am extremely committed to learning more. But this good habit had gone bad and was slowly grinding me down.

I switched to getting to work a half-hour early and reading there before I started work. Then at home, I took up reading fiction – or anything I fancied, just not work stuff.

It helped me leave work at work.

> Take a lunch break – I know, it's almost impossible as there aren't enough hours in the day anyway, right? Nope. You'll work more effectively if you take a break.

Better still, leave the building, even it's just for 5 or 10 minutes. Fresh air, walking away and some physical separation will all help you get more out of your afternoon.

I don't always manage this myself, but I do this about 3 or 4 times a week. It's a good habit.

For foster carers, try to schedule a little time just for you – take it in turns with your partner to deal with the kids, to give the other a little "me" time.

Find something that works for you… It might take a little time and creative thinking - but it's more than worth it!

ACTION POINT:

Ask yourself: which of these 3 things could you begin to do this week?

Lunch break? • Diary change? • Leaving work at work?

Rock the in-betweens

Whilst work is challenging, it does end. No charge for that one! :0)

But seriously, even if you're a foster carer, there are plenty of gaps in between the actual blocks of work itself. Making the most of these is a real help if we can pull it off.

The fast-paced, full-on, heavy duty demands of helping troubled kids means we need to make the most of the small breaks we get.

A bit like a Formula 1 car taking a pit stop...

Here are some more thoughts about how we might ensure that we take a proper break between "sessions" of work...

Pit-stop possibilities

- **Highlight achievements** – Resist the perennial obsession with criticising the caring sector. Remind yourself that the work you do makes the world a better place. What you do is worthwhile. This might help you unload the burden at the end of the working day.

- Maintain healthy boundaries – Leaving work at work is easier said than done, I know! Try making your trip home a transition point. Whenever possible, don't take work home – you really shouldn't have to. When you close your front door, shut work on the outside.

- Read your body – Take note of how you feel. If you're more tired than usual, sleeping less well, eating noticeably more or less – it's time to stop and think whether you're overdoing it. Don't automatically write it off as "understandable". Do something about it.

- Cultivate quiet – Again, easier said than done – kids, pets, family, household chores, bills, social commitments all demand attention. Try to carve out time to just "be." Stillness, peacefulness can be achieved. But we have to be deliberate. Put it in your diary and keep it free.

- DIY bath spa – You don't need a health club membership. In line with the last point, make some effort to relax regularly at home. Bubble bath, dimmed lighting, candles, soft music-or your own equivalents-can make for a half hour of stillness at any time of the day. Do what works for you.

- Get outside more – A little bit of time outdoors can clear the head. Take a walk around the block, walk to the shop, take the dog out (buy a dog!). Being outdoors helps clear the mind of its busyness. You notice more when you walk – this can be a useful distraction.

- Raise your heart rate – But not by worrying about work! The benefits of regular exercise are well established. Are you getting any? This is one of my shortcomings, too! Start small and work up – a brisk walk is better than nothing at all.

- Laugh – This helps on all kinds of levels; it's just good for the soul somehow. The associated dopamine release gives you a chemical boost too. I like Peter Kay, Michael McIntyre, Alan Partridge–buy a video. Read stuff that makes you giggle; be deliberate.

9. The great escape

Virtues of a kid-free zone

I remember my Dad telling me one day, when I was about 15, that he'd just booked a holiday. To Spain.

Now back in 1980 when a holiday for us meant a fortnight in a caravan in North Yorkshire, this was big news!

But this holiday would have even more surprises in store. What were they? Well…

No ordinary break

The big difference was – only he and Mum were going. We (the kids) were staying at home. With Aunty Linda.

Yes, you heard it right. We - that is my brother, my sister and me - weren't going. Bummer.

Now, don't get me wrong, I really liked Aunty Linda. But Spain? Not even Aunty Linda could beat that!

My parents swore by the virtues of their without-the-kids holidays. So they did it each year – a week away in September or October, to Spain, on their own. No kids.

Now I do the same.

My wife and I both work with troubled young people. Our working lives are punctuated with the kinds of information most people only hear about on the news.

We love it, but it takes its toll.

Taking a break like this has many advantages. These can be summarised in three general areas:

> Re-boot – Get a proper switch-off. When you have responsibility for children, personally and/or professionally, you always need to have some part of you focused on them.

You're always on standby. You can never fully switch off at the plug. Going away - even for a few days or a weekend - means you can. This gives your brain and body a much-needed breather from the usual vigilance that looking after children demands.

> Re-charge – Not only does this kind of time out mean you can relax, relaxing means your batteries get a proper re-charge.

You can sleep as long as you need to. Spend your days reading or climbing mountains – whatever you want to do. But only what you want to do.

I find that I sleep better and for longer. I wake relaxed because there are no obligations waiting for me in the morning. It's good for the body and good for the soul too.

> Reflect – Only when we get some distance from our normal responsibilities can we properly reflect on them. You don't have to work at this, it'll happen naturally. But only when you have some distance from it all.

And, when you're uncluttered with pressing things to do, your thoughts will be clearer and the solutions will come more easily.

You are the key

I always come back with a new clarity on where I need to make adjustments and on what I want to achieve.

This is something we all need – all the more so when we work with troubled young people.

Regardless of your professional role, and particularly as a parent, YOU are the key to helping young people.

Whether you're a...

- Residential childcare officer.

- Foster carer.

- Social worker.

- Therapist/counsellor.

- Youth worker.

- Volunteer.

- Kinship carer.

- Youth justice worker.

- Mental health worker.

- Teacher.

Or whatever...

Without you the children lose their best chance of getting the help they need. That's why you need to look after you!

10. Clinical supervision

What it is and why we need it

Even when our normal management supervision is good, it's not enough.

It's long been my contention that staff working with troubled kids – at least at the more challenging end of the spectrum – need something more.

They need clinical supervision.

What is it?

"...the formal provision, by approved supervisors, of a relationship-based education and training that is case-focussed and which manages, supports, develops and evaluates the work of junior colleagues."

(Milne, 2007:440)

Clinical supervision provides a safe and relational opportunity for us to:

- Reflect on and review our practice and the impact.

- Discuss individual cases in depth.

- Change or modify our practice and identify training and continuing development needs.

Walking through this process regularly with a trusted professional is extremely beneficial – it changed my practice for the better, quite radically.

For me – and this is just my view – the difference is about the relational quality of it and the fact that it deals with the way the person (worker) and the task (work) come together.

What it isn't

Clinical Supervision should not be confused with other "supervisory" activities, such as annual appraisal or performance review systems, or workplace mentoring.

It is also qualitatively different from the normal management or supervisory type supervision that most child care professionals get.

Here are some other things that it definitely shouldn't be…

- A people management activity allowing for monitoring of subordinates' performance.

- A forum to generate information linked to a disciplinary process.

- Mainly focused on time-keeping, workflow and/or governance.

- A punitive or gratuitously negative experience for the person being supervised.

- A continuous discussion of errors and shortcomings on the part of the employee.

Ensuring that these things don't happen is very important.

In order to achieve this it's key to get someone qualified to carry out the supervision - it's not a job for just anyone.

As well as helping to stave off burnout, there are a number of other benefits to agencies and individuals from investing in clinical supervision for staff.

Among these are:

- Improved quality of care and services.

- Professional growth and development.

- Lower sickness rates.

- A focus on clients'/patients' needs.

- Better morale.

- Reduced stress.

- Improved relationships with peers and management.

- Identification of training needs.

- Better work culture.

- Improved risk management.

- Increased staff retention.

(Source: Robinson, 2005:30)

How many more reasons does anyone need to be convinced that the benefits to staff, agency and service users are more than worth the costs?

How to do it

There are many different models and approaches to clinical supervision. Here are the main three:

- **One-to-one supervisor** (supervisor-supervised) – For me, this is the gold standard. When you get to sit with a qualified professional supervisor and talk everything through. They can guide the conversation, offer insights and/or pose questions that allow us to review and reflect on our practice.

- **Group Supervision** (supervisor-supervised group) – When a supervisor conducts discussions with a group of colleagues. There is one advantage to this – possibly two. The main one is that it's cheaper! The other is that a group conversation can directly challenge group culture, albeit in a fairly subtle way.

- **Peer Group Supervision** (dual roles: supervisors/supervised) – Again there are clear financial benefits in this approach. And though roles can more easily become blurred, this kind of clinical supervision is better than none at all. Most teams or groups of colleagues (e.g. foster carers) could quite easily convene such a forum.

N.B. Where the supervision is done in a group and/or by peers, the British Psychological Society requires a degree of one-to-one individual clinical supervision on top.

Again, this is the gold standard, but something is better than nothing, even without this backup.

Challenge to managers

As often happens, this is one area where dosh – or the lack of it – gets in the way of best practice.

Investing to save isn't a popular sport in social welfare circles - but in this case it definitely works. It takes a brave and innovative manager to bite the bullet and provide what their staff need despite the costs.

As a result most people working with troubled kids never get clinical supervision.

In desperation, some practitioners arrange and pay for their own. Most do without it altogether.

One thing is undeniable though – those working with damaged and difficult children need clinical supervision…

ACTION POINT:

Is there anything you can do as a staff member or as a manager to support colleagues more effectively?

Even if personal clinical supervision isn't an option could you try one of these other options:

Facilitated group supervision?

Peer supervision?

11. Outro

Baby steps

There is no longer any debate about whether self-care is important.

The jury has retired, deliberated and returned its verdict - we need it!

The question now is whether or not we are going to do something about our tendency to neglect our own needs.

I know that for me it took a real burnout situation to bring me up sharp so that I could see my need for this.

My plea to you is that you will act before this happens.

Action plan

As we've already said, this is not about making massive life changes overnight. Most of us can't do that.

But it is about asking ourselves some simple questions:

- What things do you already have in place to help you cope with the challenges of the work you do?

- What could you do to strengthen these and ensure you keep doing them?

- What additional small adjustment/s could you make to look after yourself better?

- Which one of these will you do this week?

- What are your warning signs that all is not well?

- Decide in advance what action you might take to stop things from escalating into ill health and absenteeism.

I wish you well in all your endeavours to help troubled kids. It is a high and worthy calling!

But in it all, don't forget to look after No. 1.

Cheers, Jonny.

If you enjoyed this little book, please leave a review on Amazon.

To get my weekly blog posts direct to your email inbox go to www.JonnyMatthew.com and enter your name and email address in the boxes provided.

Thanks!

Thank you for buying and reading this little book

The proceeds will help to keep JonnyMatthew.com as a free to access website.

Writing for my blog has been a real delight. It's been running now for a little over two years!

One of the greatest pleasures for me has been the contributions of those readers who have added their own thoughts to what I've written!

Some have commented on the posts directly. Many have been in touch via social media, whether it be Facbook, LinkedIn, Google+, Twitter or Pinterest. (Search Jonny Matthew to find me.)

Others have emailed me directly to express their views, pose their own questions or put me right when they've disagreed!

All this has added hugely to my own learning.

THANK YOU!

Bio

Jonny Matthew is currently senior adviser for effective practice at the Wales Youth Justice Board (YJB).

Prior to his current role, Jonny was a YOT practitioner for five years followed by ten years as an adolescent sexual offending specialist. In August 2013, he left his post as Interventions Lead for Hillside Secure Children's Home, and joined the YJB.

Jonny's research interests are youth crime, attachment, adoption, abuse, safeguarding and particularly how skewed developmental trajectories impact on children's behaviour and well-being.

Jonny also works on a freelance basis as a consultant social worker and criminologist. He offers consultancy, training, inspection, editing and supervision on a private basis, working with local authorities, charities and the private sector.

Jonny also runs a website and blog promoting recovery for troubled young people - www.JonnyMatthew.com

References

Milne, D. (2007) An Empirical Definition of Clinical Supervision. British Journal of Clinical Psychology, 39, 111-127

Robinson, J. (2005) Improving practice through a system of clinical supervision. Nursing Times; 101: 9, 30–32.

Copyright

Printed in Great Britain
by Amazon

69606107R00031